WORKING DOGS

Drawings by Pricilla Marden

Cover Photos: (1) Chris Luneski/Photo Researchers, (m) Maresa Pryor/Animals Animals, (r) Jim Shives/Alaska Photo

Page 5 Walter Chandoha; page 6-7 Chris Luneski/Photo Researchers; page 9 © Bill Bachman 1983/Photo Researchers; page 11 Maresa Pryor/Animals Animals; page 13 © Michal Heron 1986; page 15 © Norm Thomas 1987/Photo Researchers; page 17 Thomas Nebbia/Woodfin Camp & Associates; page 19 Rick Furniss/Wildlife Photobank/Alaska Photo; page 20-21 George Holton/Photo Researchers; page 23 Thomas Nebbia/Woodfin Camp & Associates.

Copyright © 1989 American Teacher Publications

Published by Raintree Publishers

Library of Congress number: 89-3644

Library of Congress Cataloging in Publication Data.

Marquardt, Max.
  Working dogs / Max Marquardt.
  (Real readers)
  Summary: Surveys the many tasks that dogs perform for people, for beginning readers.
  1. Working dogs—Juvenile literature. [1. Working dogs. 2. Dogs.] I. Title.
II. Series.
SF428.2.M3 1989 636.7'3—dc19   89-3644

ISBN 0-8172-3506-X

    3 4 5 6 7 8 9 0   93 92 91 90

REAL READERS

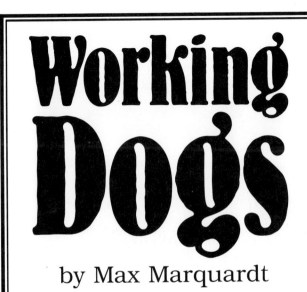

Working Dogs

by Max Marquardt

Raintree Publishers

Milwaukee

A dog can make a good pet. But there are dogs that are not pets. They are working dogs.

Working dogs can do many jobs. They do many things to help people.

Lucky is a working dog.
He helps Tom. Lucky and
Tom work with the sheep.

Little sheep are missing. Lucky finds
the sheep. He will lead the sheep back.

Bonnie is a working dog. She helps
Don. Don can't see.

Bonnie and Don go out. Bonnie leads
Don. If Bonnie stops, Don stops.
If Bonnie goes, Don goes, too.

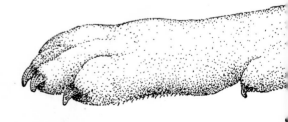

Rocky is a working dog. He works with the police. He helps stop crime.

Working dogs need to be trained
to do jobs. Rocky had to be trained
to do police work. This man helped
train Rocky to do his job.

Penny is a working dog. She helps
Ann. Ann's job
is to take newspapers
to people's homes. Penny goes with
Ann from home to home.

Koko is a working dog. She leads a team of working dogs. Koko and the team work in the snow.

Dog teams pull sleds.
They run in the snow.
In places with lots of snow,
sled dogs help people get
from place to place.

People are happy to have working dogs. Working dogs do many jobs. They help people do many things.

Sharing the Joy of Reading

Beginning readers enjoy reading books on their own. Reading a book is a worthwhile activity in and of itself for a young reader. However, a child's reading can be even more rewarding if it is shared. This sharing can enhance your child's appreciation — both of the book and of his or her own abilities.

Now that your child has read **Working Dogs**, you can help extend your child's reading experience by encouraging him or her to:

- Retell the story or key concepts presented in this story in his or her own words. The retelling can be oral or written.

- Create a picture of a favorite character, event, or concept from this book.

- Express his or her own ideas and feelings about the subject of this book and other things he or she might want to know about this subject.

Here is a special activity that you and your child can do together to further extend the appreciation of this book: You and your child can make a model out of clay of your child's favorite working dog working at its job. For example, it could be a sled dog. Make the model dog pulling the model sled. Now your child has his or her favorite working dog to view at any time.